PARKINSON
PETE'S POEMS

PARKINSON PETE'S POEMS

A collection of 20 illustrated poems

PARKINSON PETE

Illustrated by PHILIP FERGUSON JONES

Copyright © 2013 by Parkinson Pete.

ISBN: Softcover   978-1-4836-9038-4
              Ebook   978-1-4836-9039-1

All rights reserved. No part of this publication may be reproduced, stored in a retrieval system, or transmitted, in any form or by any means, electronic, mechanical, photocopying, recording or otherwise, without the permission of Parkinson Pete's Publications.

This book was printed in the United States of America.

Rev. date: 09/04/2013

To order additional copies of this book, contact:
Xlibris LLC
0-800-056-3182
www.xlibrispublishing.co.uk
Orders@xlibrispublishing.co.uk
307623

CONTENTS

Foreword 7

1. My Darling Dopamine 8
2. Poetry 10
3. Parkinson's Explained 12
4. Celebrity 14
5. Mum and Dad 16
6. Chronicity 18
7. GP 20
8. Dr Jekyll 22
9. Ted 24
10. Miracle Cure 26
11. Rumour 28
12. Juicy Steak 30
13. PD Researcher 32
14. Side Effects 34
15. Living Statue 36
16. Old Tom 38
17. Substantia Nigra 40
18. Shaking with Laughter 42
19. PD Carers 44
20. Dreams 46

FOREWORD

The purpose of writing this book of poems is to try and give the reader some insight into the world of the Parkinson's Disease patient. I have tried to do this with a mixture of humorous and serious poems so that the reader will be entertained and informed at the same time. I would like to acknowledge the enormous contribution of the illustrator, Philip Ferguson Jones, who has produced such wonderful illustrations, my daughter Anna Fargher who inspired me to write the book and gave me valuable assistance in drafting the documents and my wife Janet for her assistance in collating the book and sharing her life with me for forty years.

Parkinson Pete's Poems

My Darling Dopamine

My darling dopamine please tell me do
What it was that I did to so upset you
That you decided to slip silently away
Leaving me behind in this dreadful way

Was it the pesticide used in my teens?
Or did you not like my Parkin genes?
Was it the fact that I didn't smoke?
I know I always was an uptight bloke

Honestly it's a total mystery to me
There is definitely no family history
I just can not even begin to explain
What has happened to my poor brain

Whatever the reason can we talk?
Since you left me I can hardly walk
My life is slowly going down the pan
I am a shadow of your loving man

I know that you have heard rumours pet
That I've been knocking round with Sinemet
I can't deny it, what they are saying is true
But believe me she'll never be a match for you

If you'll come back to me my lover
I promise there will never be another
Please come back and relieve my strain
I've kept a place for you in my midbrain

There is a spot there that no other can fill
Not DBS, stem cells or even the yellow pill
Please come back to me and be my queen
My adorable, irreplaceable, dopamine

My Darling Dopamine

Parkinson Pete's Poems

Poetry

Before I published these poems for you
I asked my artistic friend to review
This book of poems for its clarity
And give me an opinion on its veracity

So my erudite friend took the book away
Promised the review the very next day
That evening he attended an academy dinner
At which he was a creative award winner

The celebrations went on very late
My friend came home in a drunken state
In his inebriation he was not able
To review my book on his bedside table

His drink fuelled brain began to dream
That he was attending a banquet supreme
He half awoke and ate a chocolate wafer
Surprisingly it tasted dry, like paper

He staggered from his bed next morning
To answer Mother Nature's urgent calling
Head pounding, mouth like cotton
Events of the night before forgotten

The job was finished, the paper work done
My friend bent to flush when his eye did run
To something floating in the bowl
He exclaimed "Well bless my soul."

What was it that my friend did see?
It looked like a line of poetry
When he recovered from his shock
My friend sat back to take careful stock

Poetry

The book, the drink, the strange food snack
  All the memories came flooding back
  What a dilemma, what could he do?
  How could he write a fair review?

Ashamed that he had let an old pal down
Because of his wild night out on the town
Then there came to him a brilliant notion
He wrote "This book was poetry in motion"

Parkinson Pete's Poems

Parkinson's Explained

Parkinson's is a complex condition
Hard to understand in our position
So to help you out I've looked it up
On the web and in a medical book

Now I'm no expert but I've done my best
To understand this veritable hornet's nest
Of deranged brain neurobiochemistry
And attempt to summarise it succinctly

In layman's terms let me spell it out
So that you know what it's all about
It all starts in the brain (that's in your head)
At least I think that's what it said

The substantia nigra, picture the scene,
It's black apparently, squirts out dopamine
Dopamine swills about and makes us fizz
It stimulates the striatum (whatever that is)

Somehow it gets itself into our muscles
Once there it sort of churns and tussles
By some enzyme bit that I'll miss out
It allows our body to easily move about

So now I hope you can understand
The workings of the normal gland
But when the whole thing goes wrong
Boy, you start to sing a different song

The substantia nigra doesn't make enough
Of the aforementioned dopamine stuff
The result of that is consequently
The muscle enzyme things are empty

Parkinson's Explained

Without the fizz they cannot work
So they go stiff and begin to jerk
So it's easy to see what produces PD
If, like me, you have studied it logically

Now that you've got an explanation
You should understand the situation
You can quote me chapter and verse
If you want to know more ask the PD nurse

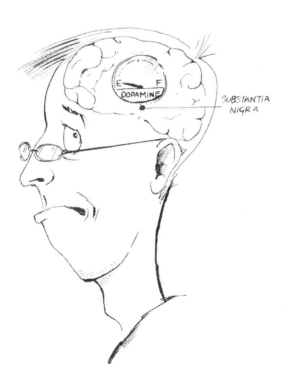

Parkinson Pete's Poems

Celebrity

When you are diagnosed with PD
You are joining a famous company
For a start there was Pope John Paul
Possibly the greatest pope of all
And let's not forget Muhammad Ali
Who floats like a butterfly and stings like a bee
Then there's Hollywood star Michael J Fox
You must have seen him on the box

As well as these people of great celebrity
The roll call also includes you and me
Why is it that we were chosen
To be slow, stiff and frozen?
Is there some great celestial plan
Or is it just the fate of man?
Will we get our reward in heaven
Did we miss selection for the first eleven?

But let us not get too downhearted
Your membership has only just started
You've years to go yet in the club
Modern treatments are very good
Instead of thinking what's gone wrong
I suggest that we are like James Bond
PD patients, I'm sure you've heard,
Are often shaken but rarely stirred

Celebrity

Parkinson Pete's Poems

Mum and Dad

I was fifty one when I got PD
I thought I should tell the family
I went to see my mum and dad
To tell them what it was I had

They were upset, it was plain to see
My mother cried then made us tea
My father, as emotional as ever
Said "Son that's not too clever"

When she had recovered from my bad news
My mother sat back and began to muse
"I'll tell you who had that" my mother said
Then she paused and scratched her head

You remember that lass from Station Street
The poor girl was a martyr to her feet
Her sister married that Yorkshire fella
The one they arrested in the King's Head cellar

Well they had a daughter, she's a bonny lass,
You know the one, she was in your brother's class
Her husband's dad had a dose of that PD
Big Irene, the caller at the bingo, told me

Her Susan knitted him a golfing sweater
You know I'm sure she said that he got better
Or did it kill him? Just a minute let me think
Was that his cousin, the plumber who mended our sink

Anyway, whoever it was, the point I'm making
Is that it doesn't have to be too life shaking
So you see son you don't need to worry
He had PD but was run over by a lorry

Mum and Dad

Parkinson Pete's Poems

Chronicity

When I joined the ranks of club PD
One thing truly astonished me
The pharmacist said I had to pay
For my medication. And the reason pray?
Because PD is not classified by those in power
As a chronic condition, what a shower!

The text book definition
Of a chronic condition
Is slow progression and long duration
Recognise the situation?
That definition seems to me
To describe PD perfectly

Deciding that PD is a condition that is not chronic
Is like saying the plague is not bubonic
Can anyone explain to me
How to justify this bizarre policy
Is there research that we have not seen
That shows recovery? Come on I mean!

PD is an incurable, progressive condition
Isn't that chronic by definition?
So come on give us all a break
It really is time to make
The one and only correct decision
And avoid our total derision
Give us our prescriptions free
Let us live in peace and chronicity

Chronicity

Parkinson Pete's Poems

GP

Spare a thought for the poor GP
Who has to deal with you and me
All the time the poor devil has got
To sort us out is a ten minute slot

Get our info up on the screen
On their inter-web machine
Read what the hospital specialist wrote
Look at the PD nurse's note

Take into account the guidance of NICE
And the practice policy on drug price
Ask us a few probing questions
Then "Have you any suggestions?"

Try and make a diagnosis
Is it PD related or neurosis?
Could it be Parkinson's psychosis?
Is that droopy eye a ptosis?

Fifteen minutes already gone
Running late, must crack on
Poor GP has not a clue
What is wrong or what to do

"I suggest that we wait and see
Come back again next Thursday
By then if it is no better
I'll write you a referral letter"

Who on earth would ever choose
To fill the poor practitioner's shoes?
I have nothing but complete sympathy
For our poor ten minute slot GP

Parkinson Pete's Poems

Dr Jekyll

The story of Dr Jekyll and Mr Hyde
To Parkinson's can easily be applied
The doctor inhabited two worlds, as do we,
We use L dopa to allow us to travel free
Between these two very different states
Interwoven, complex, linked, bedmates.

Without Parkinson pills we are like Mr Hyde
Damaged, stumbling, shaking, angry inside
But we are more like the Jekyll situation
Shortly after we have taken our medication
We can live a near normal life for many years
But gradually more and more Mr Hyde appears

We wake in the morning, disturbed inside
Definitely in the company of Mr Hyde
After breakfast pills we are in fine fettle
We are turning again into Dr Jekyll
So it continues throughout the day
First Jekyll, then Hyde, holding sway

It is a rather schizophrenic situation
To have this personality oscillation
Between our normal state of life
And the PD world of trouble and strife
In one we walk the walk just like others
In the other we become the Marx Brothers

The medication leads to a strange situation
Three times a day we see our future decrepitation
Then we get pulled back to our present state
Like twenty years has been wiped off the slate
Perhaps our story should bear a different name
Dr Jekyll and Mr Parkinson would fit the frame

Dr Jekyll

Parkinson Pete's Poems

Ted

This is the story of my best pal Ted
Whose dopamine agonist went to his head.
For his mobility it proved an undoubted saviour,
But, unfortunately, it gave him obsessive behaviour.

Ted got the urge to gamble hard
He settled on the horse racing card
Ted had been a respected university don,
In computer studies he was number one

Renowned for his academic rigour
Ted studied racing with great vigour
He immediately applied his brilliant mind
To this challenge of the equine kind

He studied jockeys, he studied courses
He studied the going, he studied horses
He studied owners, he studied stables
He recorded all the data in tables

Ted even studied race day weather
And put all the information together
He set his computer programme whirring
It worked away without Ted stirring

The programme produced, on a daily basis,
Predictions of winners in all the races.
Then what that crafty old boy Ted did
Was back each tip for fifty quid

Ted

In no time there was a veritable host
Of Ted's horses first past the post.
Money flowed in an endless stream
Ted was the cat that got the cream

Fabulously rich in his country pile
Ted sips champagne with a satisfied smile
In recognition of the money he's making
Ted's named the mansion Dunshakin

Parkinson Pete's Poems

Miracle Cure

Roll up, roll up, they're selling fast
A deal like this just will not last
Yes madam you're amazed to see
I've made a potion that cures PD
What madam you doubt my intentions?
Why I can show you my credentials
You want to see them? Not just yet
Why not madam? Because the ink's still wet.
What's in the bottles? Between you and me
I'll tell you madam if you swear to secrecy
There are flava beans from Mexico
And powerful herbs from the Orinoco,
Minerals, salts and assorted spices,
All bought for me at special prices.
Is it safe? Madam it has all been tested
In the best laboratories in West Stansted
All the evidence is posted on the Internet
Well it will be, I haven't got a website yet.
Why just yesterday I sold a man a pair
Of bottles to take home on his wheelchair.
Now swear to God and hope to die
Two hours later I saw him walking by.
I like you madam so here's what I'll do
A very special one off deal just for you.
Take these last three bottles off my hands
And I'll throw in free these two wrist bands.
They will cure arthritis, diabetes and flu.
What's that madam, it doesn't ring true?
I assure you it's the best treatment you can get
What's that? You'll stick with Sinemet.

Miracle Cure

27

Rumour

I am writing this to start a rumour
That God has got a sense of humour
When He was bored with Creation
He turned His mind to the human situation

Just for a laugh, with gay abandon
He chose some people at random
In the theatre of life to play a scene
With a diminished supply of dopamine

He didn't want a big commotion
So He directed the play in slow motion
Should He make the show a comedy?
Or perhaps it would be better as a tragedy

He could not decide which He liked the most
So He compromised and made it both
He threw in some comic touches
Wheelchairs, sticks and elbow crutches

To ensure there was no mistake
He identified the cast by their shake
To show they were serious about their lesson
He gave them all a blank expression

So you may be chosen for a starring part
In the future for this Divine new form of art
If you are selected to wear the Parkinson's gown
Remember, it is just God's way of telling you to slow down

Rumour

Parkinson Pete's Poems

Juicy Steak

Oh juicy steak how you do tempt me
How your meaty odour torments me
I long to spend the evening with you
In a cosy soirée at a table for two

I'd caress with you my knife and fork
Wouldn't bore you with inane small talk
I'd see you got the best, of course,
I'd blanket you in a pepper sauce

I'd order a bottle of the finest wine in town
Drink a large glass to wash you down
Later I'd take you back to my cosy pad
Talk all about you to my mum and dad

May I be allowed one more suggestion
A percolated coffee might aid digestion
Then off to sleep, that would be fine,
With you cuddled up in my intestine

But this dream can never come true
Alas, I can not sink my teeth in to you
Our love affair is doomed from the start
Already you have broken my poor heart

What is that makes us star crossed lovers?
That stops us from forming a union like others?
What curses us may not be obvious to see
But you've just got too much protein for me

Juicy Steak

If we shared our lives, sure, I'd be contented
But my Parkinson's drugs would be prevented
From carrying out their normal beneficial action
Leaving me frozen, stiff, in a state of distraction

So juicy steak, tragically, for you and me
This romance, unfortunately, can never be
Cruel fate with me has decided to get even
Condemning me forever to live as a vegan

Parkinson Pete's Poems

PD Researcher

I want to praise the quiet worker
My hero the PD drug researcher
Night and day they toil away
To find a cure for us one day

It is not as sexy as seeking the answer
To diabetes, heart disease or cancer
Getting funding for PD can be frustrating
Put in many bids then endless waiting

Before our heroes can begin their task
There is the ethical committee to get past
Let them study your randomised trial design?
The number needed to treat seems fine

At last the letter saying "funding approved"
And so the experiment can now be moved
Into the research laboratory active phase
Bought the kit, salaries and bills can be paid

Test tubes full of bubbling broths
Bacterial soups and chemical froths
Transgenic mice and cultured cells
Flasks full of bugs with exotic smells

Time passes and two to three years later
Our researchers have written up the paper
In a prestigious medical journal, peer reviewed,
Adds to the pool of PD knowledge accrued

PD Researcher

We hope that what these researchers will do
Is one day soon find that inspired breakthrough
That will banish for ever this cruel tyranny
And throw off the chains of our jailer PD

On behalf of the PD community I raise a glass
And propose a toast to every research lad and lass
We will support you in your brave endeavour
To find a cure and earn our gratitude for ever

Parkinson Pete's Poems

Side Effects

That good old boy the dopamine agonist
Can be both our friend and protagonist
I was due my annual PD specialist review
I knew side effects would be discussed too

I arrived at the clinic half an hour late
"Sorry, the trains are in such a state."
But to tell you the truth I had a little stop
Just down the road at the betting shop

But don't worry, I've got everything in hand
On the way home I've got things planned
I'll pop in the pub for a couple of jars
I spend a lot of time now propping up bars

Then over the road to that little Deli
With the early bird menu, I'll stuff my belly
Funnily enough while we are talking about that
The wife's been complaining that I'm getting fat

I shouldn't be telling you this, but hey,
I know you're the sort I can trust anyway
There is a massage parlour near the station
I might drop in later to ease the frustration

But let's get back to the here and now
Time for me to see the consultant, Mr Gow
We talk about things, cut down the cigarettes
Then the discussion turns to side effects

"Now then Jack, tablets giving you any bother?"
I swear to you on the grave of my mother
I was going to tell him, I was, honestly mate,
But the poor guy has got enough on his plate

Side Effects

"No Mr Gow, I've been pretty lucky that way
Apart from the expanding waist I can say
I've had no trouble with these tablets at all.
Of course I do my best to keep the dose small."

Phew that's it, I'm finished, in the clear
Won't see Mr Gow again until next year
I bet he'll ask about side effects again
Fancy a fiver on it, or maybe a ten?

Parkinson Pete's Poems

Living Statue

You must have seen those people in the street
In bizarre costume, painted from head to feet,
Standing on a box as a living statue
To try to get you to give a coin or two
The secret of success in the role they fill
Is their prolonged ability to stand stock still

I want to share with you a tricky marital situation
For which these performers were the culmination
At home, to be honest, things weren't going well
My wife and I were having the kind of difficult spell
That all PD couples periodically are subject to
When frustrations of the condition make you blue

My wife declared "I'm at the end of my tether,
We're spending too much time together.
Frankly dear you are becoming a bore
I think you really need to get out more."
That is how the whole thing began
I knew that she was hatching a plan

The very next morning as the clock struck eight
I said "Darling my tablets are not by my plate."
She smiled, "Don't worry dear, it will all be fine."
I shivered as an icy chill ran down my spine.
Because I've seen that look in her eye before
If I could move I'd have headed for the door

So it was, I swear it's true, by half past ten
My wife had me dressed and painted as a penguin.
With a Tesco trolley and two pals who popped in
She stood me on a box outside M&S with a tin
"You can have your drugs when you get home
We'll both enjoy spending some time alone."

Living Statue

So frozen in my dopamine depleted state
In trepidation I awaited my inevitable fate
Crowds gathered amazed that I stayed so still
Children were lifted up to stroke my bill
My tin filled up at such an impressive rate
That the wife had to replace it with a plate

Now I am a fixture in the shopping mall
Children can pay and be "A penguin pal"
As well as a badge and an ornate dish
Their mothers get ten percent discount on fish
To the public I am an aquatic bird serene
"Call the police!" inside my head I scream

Parkinson Pete's Poems

Old Tom

Tom went to see his GP, a doctor by the name of Rivers
Ever such a pleasant chap with an interest in the liver.
Says Tom "I'm sorry doctor to waste your precious time
But the wife says I got to tell you about these legs of mine.
They just won't go, I can't get started, I'm slowing right down.
Can't keep up with the wife, takes me ages now to walk to town."
Says Dr Rivers, "Tom there's no need to get upset or make a fuss.
There's an easy solution, when you go in to town go on the bus."

A few months later Tom was back at the practice again
"Sorry Tom, Dr Rivers is away," the receptionist did explain
So instead Tom was seen by that lovely lady, Dr Knighting.
"Doctor the wife says I got to tell you I got small writing"
Says she reassuringly, "Tom our eyesight fades as time passes.
Why don't you go down to Mr Cuthbert's and get new glasses"

The next time Tom came Dr Knighting was with child
So he saw the nurse practitioner, no nonsense Mrs Wilde
"Nurse the wife said to tell you about the mess I'm making
When I eat or drink I spill a lot 'cause my hand is shaking."
The nurse says, "Tom what age are you, seventy five,
Goodness, what else do you expect at your time of life?"

Three weeks later Tom tripped on the carpet and broke his leg
He was admitted to hospital under the care of Mr Clegg
Dr Rivers came to visit Tom in the orthopaedic ward
Says Dr Rivers, "Tom it says Parkinson's on your treatment card."
Bending down next to Tom like an old fashioned crooner
Dr Rivers said "Tom you should have come and seen us sooner."

"And that m'lud is how Dr Rivers obtained his peculiar injury.
Tom's wife says he is sorry and will replace the vase for free.
The medical report that you have seen, backed up by local talk,
Assures us it won't be long before Dr Rivers regains a normal walk.
So please m'lud and jury men, you have the facts, give it careful thought
Tom begs forgiveness and throws himself on the mercy of the court.

Old Tom

Parkinson Pete's Poems

Substantia Nigra

If you should ever chew the cud
In the neuroscientific neighbourhood
After a take away and a few beers
Out comes the wisdom of the years

Big Jed, an expert on the head,
Sighs and a tear will shed
"There is nothing so lonesome
As a broken corpus collosum"

Jackie "the syringe" McAfee
Will shake her head and disagree
"There is nothing makes me sadder
Than the poor neurogenic bladder."

I understand their point of view
But frankly, between me and you,
I hate it when the substantia nigra
Has turned into a paper tiger

It would bring a tear to anyone's eye
To learn their dopamine is running dry
PD drugs can help of course
But some would back another horse

If the substantia nigra is too lazy to work
They would stick in a wire and give it a jerk
Deep brain stimulation is the official elocution
I prefer to think of it as electrocution

I would gladly have them wire my brain
So the substantia nigra gets some pain
It's only got itself to blame, the lazy slob,
For sleeping on the dopamine job.

40

Substantia Nigra

Parkinson Pete's Poems

Shaking with Laughter

I am slow now and getting slower
I am bent now and getting lower
Sometimes I shake, sometimes I shuffle
I often freeze, can't move a muscle

I don't sleep well, I can't turn over
I'd be no good as a Casanova
My bladder tells me to go full throttle
So I always sleep with my bedside bottle

Doorways often make me freeze
Count to three and raise my knees
Protein messes with my medication
No meat, no fish, what a situation

People see me coming down the street
Shuffling, unsteady on my feet
They suspect that I've been drinking
I can see what they are thinking

They don't want me to sit near
Some make their disapproval clear
Others look away, don't make a fuss
They think "Here's the nutter on the bus"

Believe me what I say is true
Imagine if it happened to you
My life you may think is at rock bottom
But what must not be forgotten

Is I share a sense of humour with my wife
We see the funny side of PD life
That is how we stave off disaster
Every day we shake with laughter

Shaking with Laughter

Parkinson Pete's Poems

PD Carers

In this piece I would like to share
The story of those who care
For the precious PD person in their life
Be it husband, partner, friend or wife.

Whilst this condition affects them both
It is hard to say whom it hurts the most.
Alongside the many sacrifices they have made
The carer must watch their loved one slowly fade

They do their best to keep their charge safe
As together they bravely face
The inevitable progressive deterioration
It can be a heartbreak situation

Often in their twilight years
Losing touch with their peers
Together they must confront the fears,
Share the laughter and the tears.

Increasingly tethered to the home
Carers can often feel tired and alone.
Eventually the declining situation
Ends up in institutionalisation.

The carer will try and visit every day
To brighten up the inmate's stay
They find it almost impossible to pay
For a decent break or a holiday

PD Carers

So let us all join together in a toast
To salute the one we respect the most
To our companion on the road
The one who helps us bear the load

Here's to our invaluable precious carer
If only life could be just a little fairer
Please remember what they have to bear
Show our carers that you care

Parkinson Pete's Poems

Dreams

By day PD makes an old man of me
The signs are there for all to see
Of course my family and friends are fine
They offer me encouragement all of the time
But in private they shake their heads and say
"It's tragic to see him going this way."

I am a sorry shadow of a man
I try to soldier on as best I can
But at night, when I retire to my bed,
I escape to another life in my head
I leave behind this earthly PD misery
And let my spirit soar wide and free

In my dreams, no longer a figure of fun,
I dance and I leap and I walk and I run
Sometimes I relive the joys of the past
When I lived a normal life, so full and fast,
I walk once again with my wife in the Lakes
And make love in the night until day breaks

I laugh and joke with my friends at work
Respected by them, I never tried to shirk.
Then there are the dreams more offbeat
The sort that give psychologists a treat
Where I dream I can fly free in the sky
Looking down on the world from on high

All too soon I must return to earth
Stiff and sore, bladder ready to burst
To face yet another difficult PD day
Till death us do part in which I must stay
All day long I am looking forward to bed
To dream, to soar, to escape into my head

Dreams

Parkinson Pete's Poems

Printed in Germany
by Amazon Distribution
GmbH, Leipzig